MW01388025

Professor Finkel's Assignment

An Interactive Guide to The Library Room

By Kimberly Loving Ross
Assisted by Joyce Loving

Cover design for The Library Room by Carlo nino Suico

Published in the United States of America

ISBN-13: 978-1500702236
1. Fiction/Christian/General
2. Fiction/General
3. Young Adult/Spiritual
4. Educational/Religious

Acknowledgments

Thank You, God, for this opportunity to share Your word and adventure. If this work reaches the person(s) it was meant to reach, then it was worth the countless sleepless nights. May Your name be glorified. Hallelujah!

Preface

This interactive guide is designed to induce thought and conversation among friends or study partners. In most cases there are no wrong or right answers. If you discuss the questions in a group setting you may be astonished by the different views, traditions, and/or cultural differences within your near peer group. Don't judge. Don't be shocked by someone else's answers. Be brave enough to answer honestly and not what you feel others want to hear. Think for yourself. Ask God to guide your own thoughts and conclusions instead of trying to convince others of yours.

From here you'll travel the journey with Loren and her friends in their research as if you're with them.

Dear Team,

You're embarking on a journey so powerful it'll either divide or bind your group as friends forever. Each must answer the following questions: How much do I love my friends, God, and myself? Do I love my friends enough to endure hours of them challenging my beliefs? Do I love myself enough to keep an open mind in learning truths even if it goes against what I've been taught? Do I trust God enough to ask Him to show me what I need to learn and accept it? Am I brave enough to pray in my mind, and out loud? If you don't think you can, no one will think less of you if you excuse yourself from this project.

Pause here and give everyone a few moments to digest the letter, "Everyone in?"

If anyone left, judge them not. They leave knowing they've been honest and are fearful. It's no accident you were born. It's no accident you're here working on this project. It's no accident you've been invited to partake in this adventure with this particular group of people. Nothing's ever coincidental. God planned it all. Life's a test, and I pray everyone passes.

Each time you work on this project, whether alone or in a group, please bow your head and pray this prayer:

Lord, I come to You in Your special place to seek Your wisdom, to learn Your word, Your works, and Your future plans for me. Guide my lips as I speak what You need me to say, guard my mind as I discover disturbing things in Your word I wasn't prepared to read. Encourage my heart to seek You fully. Thank You for calling me to know You better. Thank You for wanting to know me. Amen.

My prayers are with you as your journey progresses.
God bless and may you pass the test by proving the truth.
Yours Truly,
Professor Jeffery Finkel

You are now a part of Loren's assignment from Professor Finkel. Class begins.

Week One

The Assignment

Day 1

Read the first chapter of The Library Room

Do you feel Jesus/Yeshua is the Messiah/Mashiach/Christ?

What have you been taught to believe?

What religion do you call yourself or follow?

When did you start learning about God?

When did you start understanding what you were learning?

Where did you learn about God?

Did you blindly accept the teachings of faith, rebel against them, or were you skeptical?

How do you feel now? (Don't write it down – just be honest with yourself.)

Are you comfortable talking about God?

Are you comfortable praying in front of others?

If you're Jewish, what do you know about Christianity other than Christians believe Jesus is the Messiah?

If you're Christian, what do you know about Judaism other than Jewish people don't believe Jesus is their Messiah?

Are you interested in learning more about the other faith?

List three things you hope to learn or gain from The Library Room & the Interactive Guide?

Day 2

Research Holidays – Holy Days

Jewish Holidays: Always start at sunset the night before, are never held on the same date every year, work is forbidden, and some last longer than what the bible says.

Christian Holidays: Always start in the morning (some consider mid-night) of the date, some are according to lunar calendar (example – Easter) while others are always on the same date every year (example – Christmas,) work is forbidden, and it is just for one day.

The following holiday list is more commonly observed by the American Jewish people. Please research the holidays and become familiar with the timing, length, and reason. This is not a complete list of their religious holidays; however, these are the holidays they expect you to know. Depending upon whom you ask, or what sect a Jewish person belongs to, will determine the length of the holiday – traditions and cultures vary. The date is always the same every year according to the JEWISH CALENDAR (lunar.) Keep in mind; even though it says it's celebrated on a certain day, it actually begins at sundown the day before.

Passover – Starts _____ day of _____ (Jewish Lunar Calendar) and ends _____.
Starts on _____ (Common Calendar) and ends _____ this year.
What happens during this holiday?
When did it start being observed?

Rosh Hashanah – Starts _____ day of _____ (Jewish Lunar Calendar) and ends _____.
Starts on _____ (Common Calendar) and ends _____ this year.
What happens during this holiday?
When did it start being observed?

Yom Kippur - Starts _____ day of _____ (Jewish Lunar Calendar) and ends _____.
Starts on _____ (Common Calendar) and ends _____ this year.
What happens during this holiday?
When did it start being observed?

Chanukah - Starts _____ day of _____ (Jewish Lunar Calendar) and ends _____.
Starts on _____ (Common Calendar) and ends _____ this year.
What happens during this holiday?
When did it start being observed?

Sukkot – Starts _____ day of _____ (Jewish Lunar Calendar) and ends _____.
Starts on _____ (Common Calendar) and ends _____ this year.
What happens during this holiday?
When did it start being observed?

Shavu'ot – Starts _____ day of _____ (Jewish Lunar Calendar) and ends _____.
Starts on _____ (Common Calendar) and ends _____ this year.
What happens during this holiday?
When did it start being observed?

Here is a list of the most common Christian holidays celebrated in America. Although some may not be as popular as others due to sects, traditions, and European cultures, they are listed because more than ten percent of the Christian population in America observes the holiday.

Epiphany – Celebrated on _____ (Common Calendar).
What happens during this holiday?
When did it start being observed?

Mardi Gras – Starts _____ day of _____ (Lunar Calendar) and ends _____.
Starts on _____ (Common Calendar) and ends _____ this year.
What happens during this holiday?
When did it start being observed?

Ash Wednesday – Starts _____ day of _____ (Lunar Calendar) and ends _____.
Celebrated on _____ (Common Calendar).
What happens during this holiday?
When did it start being observed?

Good Friday – Starts _____ day of _____ (Lunar Calendar) and ends _____.
Celebrated on _____ (Common Calendar).
What happens during this holiday?
When did it start being observed?

Easter – Starts _____ day of _____ (Lunar Calendar) and ends _____.
 Starts on _____ (Common Calendar) and ends _____ this year.
What happens during this holiday?
When did it start being observed?

St. Patrick's Day – Celebrated on _____ (Common Calendar).
What happens during this holiday?
When did it start being observed?

St. Valentine's Day – Celebrated on _____ (Common Calendar).
What happens during this holiday?
When did it start being observed?

Halloween – All Hallows Eve, All Hallows, and All Souls (hint – technically three days) Starts on _____ (Common Calendar) and ends _____ this year.
What happens during this holiday?
When did it start being observed?

Christmas – Celebrated on _____ (Common Calendar).
What happens during this holiday?
When did it start being observed?

Should Jewish holidays stop being observed by Christians?

Do you feel the American society observes Christian holidays in a sacred manner as they do Jewish holidays?

Do you celebrate the Christian holidays as a Christian the way it was *intended*?

How much paganism has been allowed into the celebration traditions of both religions?

How did paganism infiltrate religious Holy Days?

Why do you feel Christianity was more tolerant of the pagan rituals infiltrating into the celebrations?

Day 3

Read Tanakh, Torah, Genesis 2:2 & 3, Tanakh, Torah, Exodus 20:8 - 11, & then New Testament, Hebrews 4:1 - 11

Is Shabbat/Sabbath still important?

Do you observe it regularly?

Does it matter which day of the week?

Is it okay to allow aliens (illegal or legal) to do work for us on Sabbath?

Do you feel corporations and society are diluting the need or practice of resting on Sabbath/Shabbat?

Why is it important to make a day of rest?

How do you feel the day of rest as a Hebrew or Christian is different than others?

In the past when you've focused on God during your day of rest did you feel more rested? (Yes - completely, Never really noticed, or No - no difference)

What do you do to rest and spend time with God on your Shabbat/Sabbath?

What can you do to make your Shabbat/Sabbath more "restful" so you can feel God's intended grace and peace?

Day 4

Read the Second Chapter of The Library Room

Why are you here on Earth?

Why are you participating in this interactive guide?

What do you think your purpose is on earth?

Why didn't God make and keep us in Heaven instead of sending us to earth first? (Keep in mind, different beliefs are just that. Don't judge or try to persuade your opinions on others. Only share your belief and see how it is different.)

Do we really need a purpose?

Is our purpose the same as "a calling?"

What is your calling?

How does your calling and/or purpose relate to God's plans?

We'll be coming back to these questions later in the study. This exercise was to get you to thinking about where you're seeing yourself and your connection with God's intentions.

Day 5

Read Chapter Three in The Library Room (read Genesis chapters 1 – 22 to verify research if needed.)

Why do you feel the first three chapters in the Torah are important for you to know?

Do you believe everything happened just as it says?

Write Tanakh, Torah, Genesis 3:15 -19 in your own words – summarize it.

Why is this verse important to know?

What was the only way you could approach God after Adam and Eve sinned by eating the forbidden fruit?

First Cain disobeyed parental instruction of proper sacrificial procedures (strong willed ego.) Then he ignored God's warning to get it right, stop being jealous, and not let the pity party turn into rage over his own poor decision (pity, ego, arguing with authority, rebelling.) And then ultimately Cain killed his brother, Abel, out of rage and jealousy. What were the consequences of Cain's sins?

How do you think Adam and Eve felt when their son, Cain, was evicted from their home as they'd been evicted from their home in the Garden of Eden?

How do you think Adam and Eve felt knowing their sins had caused the corrupt nature in the souls of their children?

Do you feel it is coincidental that names were recorded before anyone knew they'd be needed to verify a bloodline linking to the Messiah?

Are the sons or descendants of Ishmael recorded in fine detail as his brother Isaac's? (Islam believes Muhammad is a descendant of Ishmael and so does Baha'u'llah of the Bahá'í religion.)

Are the sons or descendants of Esau's recorded in detail?

Considering Abraham was born two thousand years before Yeshua/Jesus, how did they know to continue recording along the selective lineage?

Why do you think God had all the names recorded and then added unique details when needed about closed womb miracles? (i.e.: First Abraham & Sarah, then her son Isaac's wife Rebekah, and then their son and daughter-in-law, Jacob & Rachel.)

What was the importance of pointing out the miracle births that occurred two thousand years before Jesus's?

What does the lesson about the mandrakes with Rachel indicate about God and superstitions?

Did you notice Rachel did not conceive until she began praying to God instead of her father's idols?

Week Two

Lineage & Birth Prophecies

Day 1

Read Chapter Four and Five of The Library Room

Do you feel it was okay for the Christians to rearrange the Scripture books in the Old Testament?

Do you feel it really matters to you personally?

Do you feel it may discourage Jewish people from continuing onto the New Testament?

Did you grow up learning the books of the Tanakh (Old Testament?)

Why do some Christian Bibles include more books than others?

How often do you typically read scriptures?

Are you willing to commit to reading scriptures daily?

Before reading scriptures ask God to forgive your sins and guide your mind as to where He wants it to go.

What does the Bible say about drunkenness? Let's find out... Did you know there are over 80 scriptures pertaining to the word "drunkenness" in the Holy Bible? Both the Tanakh and New Testament have scriptures warning us of the dangers.

Read the following verses: Ephesians 5:18, Proverbs 20:1, Galatians 5:19-21, Luke 21:34, Isaiah 28:7, I Timothy 5:23, Proverbs 3:20-35, Romans 13:13, Jeremiah 25:27, Isaiah 5:11 – 22, I Corinthians 6:10, Hosea 4:11, I Thessalonians 5: 7-8, Habakkuk 2:15-17, Proverbs 21:17, Proverbs 23:21, Romans 14:21, Nahum 1:10

What is your opinion regarding alcoholic beverage consumption, smoking marijuana, or other "recreational" drugs (other than for medical purposes)?

Do your opinions differ from the above scriptures?

In Galatians 5:19-21 – It's human nature to read those scriptures and think, "I don't do that one...not guilty of that one...oops, I'll need to work on that one...but, I don't do that one – too often..." Isn't it funny how our egos will soften our spankings when we're confronted with God's words?

Anyone who knows me knows I am the queen of finding loopholes. I'd learned way back in the eighties while working as a travel agent that there is no such thing as a problem once you find the creative loophole. (The travel industry with their fare rules turned us all into loophole finding fiends to stay competitive.)

So I looked again while asking, "What does that list mean?" Are they really as evident as it says?

Sexual immorality is self explanatory. I'm sure we're all guilty of that to a certain degree. We live in America – the most promiscuous nation in the world…well, one of them. And if that little phrase didn't make it clear then "sensuality, orgies, and *things like these*" should cover any loophole you'll try to find to justify or get away with such actions.

If you highlight "impurity" and clicked on synonyms you'll see it means unclean, dirty, corrupted, etc. If you're walking around with an unclean spirit dirtied from sin that's impurity. If you don't want forgiveness for a certain sin because you feel you were justified in committing it; that's impurity.

Idolatry isn't just a figurine or knick-knack a person prays to for power or serenity. Idolatry adores things/items/persons that make you feel good or give you power – money, cars, yourself, your job, jewelry, houses, drugs, clothing, rock stars, sports stars, crystals for different luck or powers, etc… A lot of people will do harmful things to themselves or others to promote, obtain, or be near such idols. Note: *If you spend more time obsessing over it than you do God chances are it's a hidden idol in your life.*

Sorcery, witchcraft, fortunetelling, mind controlling, all fall under the "and things like these." If you're looking for an answer or power by bypassing God there are no loopholes for permission to do so…sorry.

Enmity, strife, jealousy, fits of anger, rivalries, dissensions, divisions, envy, and "things like these," all seem to fit together. Enmity is hostile, hatred, and bitterness. Strife is causing conflict, dissention, bean-stirring, and drama. Jealousy is often the cause of enmity, strife, fits of anger, and rivalries. Rivalries, strife, and jealousy always cause dissensions, divisions, and "things like these."

Drunkenness will most often lead a person to do all those things above as well as the "things like these."

To clarify, God severely opposes those specific things mentioned. We forfeit our inheritance in the Kingdom of God over doing those things and the "things like these." I can't find any loopholes. This list can be found throughout the entire Tanakh and New Testament. Why?!

God wants us to look to *Him* for all good things. He knows we'll have needs. Ask Him to supply them. He knows we'll fall short of His rules, especially the ones above. Don't let it become an impurity issue. Ask Him to help you overcome those obstacles and ask for forgiveness. (He makes it easy to do so.)

It's quite simple in the end and not so scary when you know we have a forgiving God and that He is bigger than those issues. Take time to talk to God about them today. Don't delay.

How many of those items are you dabbling in or have dabbled in without realizing it is a sin?

Day 2

Read Chapter Six and Seven of The Library Room

During the Period of Enlightenment, what was the popular belief?

Other than being mentioned earlier in the interactive guide, have you ever wondered why we're here?

Have you ever wondered how you fit in with God's big plan?

Do you feel God has a big plan?

If yes, why do you feel so?

Do you feel God hears your individual prayers?

Share with the group a time (if you have one) when you've felt God was listening to your prayers, thoughts, or requests.

Growing up Christian or Jewish did you ever feel slighted because of your beliefs?

Did your school celebrate your holidays or holidays of other religions?

Did you feel left out *or* acknowledge those who were being left out?

Has the "politically correct" movement in America had an effect on people praying over their meals in public?

How do you feel about praying in public over your meals?

Do you feel some people become uncomfortable observing our prayers to God? If so, why?

Have you ever prayed in public other than over your meal?

If yes, were you able to stay focused *or* were you, in the back of your mind, wondering what people around you were thinking?

Do you care if someone is offended by your praying in public?

While you're praying out loud do you worry about how you sound to the people around you more than how you sound to God?

Think of something that has been on your mind this past week. Tell the group what has been occupying your thoughts. After you've explained your concern, pray over it out loud.

As you've heard others in the room sharing and praying over their own concerns did you feel uncomfortable?

Your challenge is to begin praying in public silently or out loud.

Day 3

Read Chapter Eight of The Library Room

List at least two different miracle births that have happened in the Tanakh/Old Testament.

How important were those births in the lineage of David?

Do you feel the recording of miracle births was a coincidence in regards to Jesus's own miraculous birth?

Why were the story's of the miracle births explained in detail; while, normal births were blips in the Tanakh?

Is it a coincidence that there were so many miraculous births prior to Jesus's birth in that bloodline?

You've read the story summarized by the friends in The Library Room – now, with your group read Tanakh, Nevi'im, Isaiah 4:2, Tanakh, Nevi'im, Jeremiah 23:5-6, Tanakh, Nevi'im, Isaiah 7:14, and Tanakh, Nevi'im, Micah 5:2.

Have two people from the group take turns reading the following verses in order. Luke 2:1-7, Matthew 2:1-8, Luke 2:8-39, Matthew 2:9-12.

Summarize: Tanakh, Nevi'im, Malachi 3:1-5, Tanakh, Nevi'im, Malachi 4:5, Tanakh Nevi'im, Isaiah 40:3

Day 4

Read Chapter Nine and Ten of The Library Room

Name at least two wars that were results of different religious beliefs.

There are still wars involving genocide occurring today as a result of religious beliefs. How often do you hear about them in the news?

Research the countries currently persecuting Jews and Christians (Hint: there are over 45 nations out of 221.) Select a country to pray for for the rest of the year.

In your research, did you find a/the wars were strictly religiously motivated?

Were money or resources (mineral rights, waterways, grazing lands, etc.) a factor in any way?

Research the ancestors of your religious sect. Were there any historical evil characters that blemished the denomination's reputation?

How do you think Satan has used those characters to discredit God's people and religions of faith?

Have you ever shied away from going to a certain church or synagogue as a result of past extremists, a sinful fall of a person in a high position, or historical evil characters?

How do you know the difference between a good and bad church or synagogue? (This is your opinion; there is no right or wrong answer.)

Day 5

Read Chapter Eleven and Twelve of The Library Room

Have you ever become angry at God because you believed He ignored your prayers?   Are you still angry or disappointed?

On the occasions you'd given up on your own will, how did you convince yourself to let it go and trust God's plans or timing?

Have you ever been on the hurting side of a failed relationship? (This does not have to mean romantically.)

Was it your fault?

Does it still hurt?

Did you blame God?

Have you forgiven the other person or asked for forgiveness?

What are abusive behaviors in a relationship?

Do you feel society uses "abuse" as a convenient excuse for considering divorce and giving up on a relationship? Explain.

In the last few pages of Chapter Twelve of The Library Room, Officer Scott Jones asks Loren questions concerning her relationship with Giles to make her understand that she's in an abusive relationship.

Warning signs of an abusive relationship:

- ✓ Complete control or manipulation of money
- ✓ Topics you cannot discuss
- ✓ Limitation on whom you may see or how long you may be with your friends
- ✓ Limitation of where you're allowed to go
- ✓ Blaming of bad behavior or negative reactions
- ✓ Belittles your accomplishments
- ✓ Makes you feel like you're the crazy one in the relationship
- ✓ You suspect the other person is chemically unbalanced
- ✓ Stalks or checks up on you out of fear
- ✓ Easily subjected to jealousy
- ✓ Threatens to hurt you or your loved ones if you don't obey
- ✓ Forces sex

✓ Has apologized or apologizes for physical outburst – hitting/kicking you or throwing objects

Do you feel there should have been more questions added to Officer Jones' list?

Do you feel some of the questions are out of line and don't really constitute abuse?

Have you ever been in an abusive relationship?

If yes, how long did it take you to realize your situation was abusive?

Do you feel abusive relationships will escalate over time *or* should be worked out through counseling?

Have you ever helped a friend realize or escape from an abusive relationship?

What can you do to prevent yourself from becoming a victim of an abusive relationship?

Have you ever prayed for someone you didn't like?

Your challenge is to pray for a personal enemy over the next 90 days. Write that person's name on a separate piece of paper and place it inside your Tanakh or Holy Bible with the words "pray for healing and forgiveness." At the end of the 90 day period if you do not have forgiveness keep praying until you can look at that name and not feel resentment.

What if they are deceased? Pray for God to help you forgive them completely so when you see that name and visualize their face you are no longer resentful.

Read, Tanakh, Ketuvim, 2 Chronicles 7:14, Tanakh, Nevi'im, Micah 7:18-19, Tanakh, Nevi'im, Daniel 9:9, New Testament , 2 Corinthians 2:5-7   New Testament, Matthew 6:9 – 18, New Testament, Matthew 18:23 – 35,

If you look up the word "FORGIVE" on BlueLetterBible.com you will see that word is in the bible 56 times in 48 verses. That is just for the word "forgive." It doesn't include the words, "forgiven," "forgiveness," or "forgave." God tells us it's important for us to understand forgiveness here on Training Camp Earth.

Week Three

Yeshua's Miraculous Birth

Day 1

Read Chapter Thirteen of The Library Room

Compare Tanakh, Nevi'im, Hosea 11:1 – 4 to Matthew 2:10 – 18

How does Jesus' birth compare to stories you see on television or in plays?

Did you notice the word "child" versus "baby" in Matthew 2:11?

Where did the Kings meet up with Joseph, Mary, and Jesus?

How old was infant Jesus at the time of that meeting and gift giving?

Why do you feel the Christmas story is typically cut short after the Kings give their gifts and does not include Joseph fleeing with his family to Egypt that same night?

Is the fleeing to Egypt piece of the story an important part of fulfilling prophecy?

Tanakh, Nevi'im, Jeremiah 31:35, New Testament, Matthew 2:18

If prophesies are echoed (prophesied more than once) such as it is the second time in Tanakh, Torah, Chukat-Balak, Numbers 23:21-22, do you consider that to be a strong clue from God to keep a watch for it?

If you disagree, why do you feel it is not?

Another echoed prophecy is Tanakh, Nevi'im, Jeremiah 23: 5 - 6 and Tanakh, Nevi'im, Jeremiah 33:14 – 16. How did Jesus fulfill these prophecies?

It's important to know how the Messiah needs to come out of Bethlehem, Jerusalem, and Egypt. Where does Muhammad (Islam) come from?

Where does Baha'u'llah come from?

Where does Buddha come from?

Are there more prophecies that still need to be fulfilled?

If so, which ones?

Was Christ perfect and righteous?

Was Moses?

Was Muhammad?

Was Baha'u'llah?

Was Buddha?

Research the prophecies Tanakh, Nevi'im, Isaiah 53: 2 – 12 one section at a time and discuss with the group. Use scriptures to support your findings. You may use The Library Room as a source of reference on this portion or utilize your own source of research references.

What is the significance of John the Baptizer (Yochanan) baptizing Jesus?

What was the significance of Jesus being baptized?

What did God do the moment Jesus was baptized?

Should adults continue to be baptized or use a mikveh?

Did Jesus baptize babies or adults? John 3:22 – 36

What did Jesus do with children? New Testament, Mark 10:13 - 15

Have you been baptized?

If you have, was it as a child or as an adult?

Day 2

Read Chapter Fourteen in The Library Room

How much control do you allow others to have over you?

Describe what you feel is an acceptable form of control, manipulation, or compromise.

When is manipulation, control, or compromising, not acceptable?

"How important is it?" is a slogan many people use throughout their day to help guide their level of arguing. Our egos tell us it's vital we're to be understood and we're right. However, in doing so we neglect how others around us may feel about being heard and understood.

Read: Tanakh, Nevi'im, Jeremiah 48:29-30, New Testament, II Corinthians 12:20

Do you know someone who feels they're always right?

How does that person make you feel while spending time with them?

How often do you concede to someone else's views?

How often are you demanding others to see things your way?

What did you think about Mitch's telephone conversation with his daughter, Loren?

In your study group stand, hold hands, and each take a different area of influence regarding your life: the new or changing government laws, current government laws, peers, relationships, church/synagogue teachings, family members, and God. Ask God to place you where you need to be in accordance to His plans and those areas.

Commit to each other to pray to God to have more control over your life and to guide your thoughts, missions, agendas, what you say to others, relationships, and your future.

Were any of those areas hard to release power to God instead of keeping control over it yourself?

Describe spiritual warfare:

Have you experienced a time when you've gained additional knowledge (other than what you initially set out to learn) when you're looking up information while working on this guide?

Do you feel God was guiding you to know more on a subject even if it wasn't directly related to what you were looking up at the time?

Have any of the members of your group experienced spiritual warfare since beginning this study guide?

Are any in need of prayer to overcome the distraction?

Look up the covenant God delivered to the Hebrews on Mount Sinai. What does it entail specifically?

Law: Tanakh, Torah, Exodus 20:1 -17,
Tanakh, Torah, Exodus 24:3-8
Condition of the Law:

Were there more laws (Mitzvot) added later?

Rewards and punishments of keeping God's Laws (Mitzvot)

Read Deuteronomy 11 - Deuteronomy 28:

Rewards: Punishments:

Would or could God recant His offer given in the covenant delivered at Mount Sinai?

Should He?

Does the Covenant assure salvation?

What is typology?

How hard would it be for anyone to use the Tanakh scriptures to justify themselves as a Mashiach?

Has it been done before?

Do you believe the Messianic prophecies, or do you feel all of them are coincidental at this point in the research?

Day 3

Read Chapter Fifteen in The Library Room

What do you *think* the bible says about premarital sex (also known as fornication?)

New Testament, 1 Corinthians 7:2

It's important to note the biblical definition of fornication specifically indicates sex between an unmarried/non-engaged man and an unmarried/non-engaged woman. The mainstream dictionary definitions of fornication include: seduction, rape, sodomy, bestiality, prostitution, homosexuality, and incest. The biblical definition does *not* include sexually immoral acts.

Do you feel this is important to know?

According to biblical terms an unmarried person is a virgin/never been married, widow/widower, or divorcee.

Read New Testament, Galatians 5:19 and New Testament, Hebrews 13:4

The scriptures clarify the differences between fornication and adultery.

Is this important to know?

The Greek words "porneia" (noun) and "porneuo" (verb) relate to consensual sex between a single man and a single woman. It does not include sexually immoral (unnatural sexual acts such as harlotry, prostitution, sodomy, homosexuality, perversion, etc.) So again, we'll point out that throughout biblical translations since there wasn't a proper one-word translation for "sexually immoral" the word "fornication" was often used; or rather misused. An example would be: New Testament, 1 Corinthians 5:1

What does the bible say about marital cheating also known as adultery?

Tanakh, Torah, Leviticus 20:10
New Testament, Mark 10:11

What does Hollywood and the music industry convey to society about premarital sex and/or adultery?

What does your church/synagogue family say about premarital sex?

How is premarital sex viewed in other countries?
France
Ireland
Russia
Iran
India
China
Australia
Brazil
Egypt

How much pressure do people face in today's society to engage in premarital sex?

Tanakh, Torah, Exodus 22:16-17, Tanakh, Torah, Deuteronomy 22:22-29

What were the consequences of fornication in biblical times?

What was the consequence if one was engaged or already married?

What were the consequences of adultery in biblical times?

What was the consequence of rape in biblical times?

What are the consequences of premarital sexual relationships for young adults in America or western countries?

What are the consequences of adultery or premarital sex in America?

What are the consequences of premarital sexual relationships for older adults/widows/widowers/divorcees?

What is Shomer Negiah?

Do you feel there is a reason for Shomer Negiah to regain popularity among our faithful youth?

Is Shomer Negiah practiced more in other faiths or regions than your current faith and region?

What does 1 Corinthians 6:19 – 10 say about our bodies?

Day 4

Read Chapter Sixteen regarding "The Twelve Tribes" from The Library Room

Who started the Zionist movement?

When did it start?

Why did it start?

What is the meaning of Jacob's name?

What is the meaning of Israel's name?

Who were the original twelve tribes and when were they created? Tanakh, Torah, Vayishlach, Genesis 35:23-26, Tanakh, Torah, Shemot, Exodus 1:1-5, Tanakh, Torah, Bamidbar, Numbers 1:20-43 and Tanakh, Ketuvim, 1 Chronicles 2:1-2

Why weren't the Levites given their own portion?

Why aren't the original twelve tribes the same as the twelve tribes that entered into The Promised Land?

Read Tanakh, Neviim, Isaiah 43. How does this prophecy fit with the return of the tribes?

Day 5

Read Chapter Seventeen and Eighteen of The Library Room

If you'd been in Loren's shoes, how might you have treated Mellissa when she returned your stolen items?

What type of greeting do you think Mellissa expected when she returned the items?

Have you ever been the victim of being used by someone to instigate a vengeful act?   Explain.

Did you apologize or were you too embarrassed?

What does God say about gossip?   Tanakh, Ketuvim, Proverbs 6:16-19, Tanakh, Ketuvim, Proverbs 21:23, Tanakh, Ketuvim, Psalms 34:13, Tanakh, Torah, Exodus 23:1, New Testament, James 1:26, New Testament, Matthew 12:36, New Testament, James 3:8

How does gossip affect a church body?

"In life you're either doing God's will or being Satan's pawn." Mr. O'Mallee, Loren's landlord.

What do you think of this saying?

How often do you justify riding the fine line of right and wrong?

Do you feel the current research we've done so far in this study has been biased?

If yes, what objectives do you feel haven't been brought up yet?

Are there two different ways to get to heaven?

Do Jews need a Messiah to get to Heaven/Olam HaBa?

What do you call Heaven or the afterlife?

Josephus, Thallus, Mara Bar-Serapion, weren't pro-Christian so they're not in the Bible yet they provide witness to critical events. Why is it important to know there are non- Biblical and Jewish records of Jesus's life, crucifixion, resurrection, and ascension?

What other documents or artifacts can be found to validate the events?

Why aren't they discussed often?

Is it human nature to not want to believe in Jesus or God? Why?

What does the word "faith" mean to you?

Have you ever felt like God was speaking to you?

Do you talk to God throughout the day in your mind?

Describe what Catholics consider "accidents."

Describe what Catholics feel happens during transubstantiation.

Why aren't all ministers, priests, pastors, or preachers, capable of transforming wine and bread into the actual blood and flesh of Jesus?

Was transubstantiation always a part/belief of the Catholic Church?

When did it start?

What was the political environment like at the time?

Did all the priests agree with the act?

When did the Protestant movement begin?

Did transubstantiation have anything to do with the apostasy of Protestantism from Catholicism?

When did you understand communion or your relationship with God and the act of communion?

How old do you feel you need to be in order to understand your relationship fully with God?

Week Four

The Moses Comparison & Holy Spirit

Day 1

Read Chapter Nineteen of The Library Room

Write and memorize: Tanakh, Torah, Deuteronomy 18:15

Write and memorize: New Testament, John 5:45-47

Speculate as to why God would tell Moses to prophesy Deuteronomy 18:15 after He'd already given the Hebrews the covenant at Mount Sinai?

What are the odds of both Moses and Jesus being survivors of Kings demanding infanticide?

Is/was that a common act – to kill all male babies or babies in general?

The book of James was written by Jesus's half brother who at one time "misunderstood" His calling. How hard would it be to believe your half-brother is the Messiah even though you've grown up witnessing his flawless and faultless character?

When you read the miracles of both Moses and Jesus, keep in mind these few things: *Both* always gave credit to God for producing the miracle, *both* performed God's miracles in front of several to millions of people at a time, and *both* were written about outside of scriptures – not just folklore or embellishments. There are several artifacts recording such happenings in art and documents.

While visiting Nuweiba, Egypt, in 1978 Ron Wyatt discovered artifacts of Moses' crossing at the bottom of the Red Sea. His first discovery was coral encrusted human and horse bones along with chariot remains. Other divers have found remains off of the Saudi coastline as well. The span between Egypt and Saudi in that particular pathway is about eleven miles and crosses along an underwater "hillcrest."

His second discovery was a column pillar in the waters with eroded inscriptions off of the coast of Nuweiba, Egypt, near the hillcrest and the coral encrusted remains.

His third discovery in 1984 was a second identical column off of the Saudi coast in line with the hillcrest and first column. Some of the inscriptions were still legible. It included words in archaic Hebrew: Moses, Solomon, Pharaoh, Mizraim (Egypt,) Edom, death, and Yahweh. This column has since been replaced by a flag marker by the Saudi government.

It is believed King Solomon had the two columns placed at the two locations as a memorial.

King Solomon had set these columns as a memorial to the miracle of the crossing of the Israelites.

Why do you feel this information isn't publicized more in the media or history books?

Would this be proof positive of God's power and miracles or would people need more proof of His existence?

Was there still proof of what had happened to the Hebrews during the time of establishing the Israelites?

Do we need updated proof of God's existence to prove He's still here?

If He's not still here where did He go?

Were the miracles Yeshua performed another way of letting the Israelites know He's still God, still exists, and always will exist?

Do you know of, or have you experienced a miracle you'd like to share with the group?

Can you think of other ways Jesus and Moses were alike?

Have you ever researched other prophets or religions resulting from Abraham's lineage (Islam, Bahá'í, or others?)

How do they match up against the Moses Comparison prophecy?

Findings of the Red Sea Discoveries may be found at:
www.snopes.com/religion/redsea.asp
www.truthorfiction.com/rumors/c/chariot-wheels.htm#.U9-YwvldW8o

Day 2

Read Chapter Twenty and Twenty-One of The Library Room

Have you ever been awaken from sleep with an urge to pray? If so, explain.

What is fasting?

What does your church/synagogue teach regarding fasting with prayer about important issues?

Have you ever fasted and prayed about a situation?

Read: Tanakh, Nevi'im, Joel 2:12,
Tanakh, Nevi'im, Isaiah 58:4,
New Testament, Matthew 6:16-18

Share with the group your favorite scripture verse(s) you reflect upon during times of stress or need.

Since starting the Interactive Guide, have your, individually or as a group experienced spiritual warfare?

Has it been difficult to attend the meetings?

How do you feel about the material and research done so far? Share with your study group.

Do you believe Jesus is the Messiah?   Is there anyone in your group who does not believe He could be the Messiah?

Are there still some areas of concern from you or anyone in your group?

Do the Jewish people need a Mashiach *or* do you feel the covenant is enough for them?

Do you feel Jewish people need a different Mashiach because God keeps them different?

Is the Spirit of God in the Tanakh the same as The Holy Spirit in the New Testament?

Do they behave the same?

What age were you when you became aware of God and the need to repent?

How old were you when you celebrated your Confirmation/Being Saved/Bar Mitzvah/Bat Mitzvah?

What was it like?

Did you and your family have an elaborate celebration?

Do you feel that step in your life is worthy of an elaborate celebration?

What is sin?

What is sin doing to your relationship with God?

Are you comfortable speaking or praying to God if you haven't asked Him for forgiveness?

Does He hear your prayers if you have unresolved sin issues *or* is it a wedge between you two?

Research the Ashamnu, and Teshuvah, Jewish prayers (or share with the group if you're Jewish/Messianic.)

Read Tanakh, Nevi'im, Daniel 9.
How do you feel when you read the confessional prayers?

Do you feel Christianity has softened the humbling procedure of repenting?

Pray the sinner's prayer as Amy instructed Amelia to do.
Did you feel a difference? Explain one way or the other.

Was it God's intention to make repentance easier by not having to sacrifice an offering since Yeshua became the ultimate sacrifice?

Does this mean we should take for granted our confessions will be forgiven with a simple prayer?

Why should Christians go back to traditional ways of praying and confessing guilt *or* should they?

Do you have unresolved forgiveness with a family member or former friend?

Is it possible to ask them to forgive you?

Do you feel they deserve to know that you're sorry?

What if the shoe were on the other foot – would you forgive them?

Have you ever felt as if a wedge develops between you and God when you go days without praying or asking for forgiveness?

Does this compare with the relationship between you and God?

How do you forgive someone who has done evil to you or a loved one?

Is it important to forgive someone face to face who has done extreme evil?

Have you ever lead anyone astray from God?

How did you feel at the time?

Have you ever lead anyone astray from accepting Yeshua?

How did you feel at the time?

Day 3

Read Chapter Twenty-Two of The Library Room

Read Tanakh, Torah, Exodus 19:3-6
Is this a conditional covenant?

What are the conditions?

Read New Testament, Matthew 27:50
What significant things happened when Jesus took His last breath on the cross?

How many saw these things happen?

Read Tanakh, Nevi'im, Isaiah 44:3, Tanakh, Nevi'im, Ezekiel 39:29, and Tanakh, Nevi'im, Joel 2:28-29

Were/are the Hebrews expecting the arrival and indwelling of the Holy Spirit to all?

Read New Testament, Luke 24:50-53, and New Testament, Acts 2:1-41

What significant things happened after Jesus ascended?

Is God and His Holy Spirit one in the same?

Read New Testament, Acts 1:3-5

How long did Jesus walk the earth after He was raised from the grave but before He ascended?

How is this different from Hollywood's stories?

Was He seen by just the twelve disciples *or* many others?

Why is it important to know He was on earth for more than a month, eating, teaching, and being seen by so many before His ascension?

Why don't Christians have a Holy Day fifty days after Passover to celebrate Pentecost (The day of first fruits as observed by Judaism) since the Holy Spirit came and indwelled in all on that day?

Read Tanakh, Nevi'im, Isaiah 44:3-6, Tanakh, Nevi'im, Isaiah 61:1-3, New Testament, John 7:37-39, New Testament Acts 1:5, Tanakh, Nevi'im, Joel 2:28-29, New Testament Acts 16:7-9, New Testament, Acts 22:30, New Testament, Romans 8:2-27, New Testament, 1 Corinthians 2:6-16, New Testament, Ephesians 4, New Testament, Galatians 5:22-23

What are some of the effects we may experience from the Holy Spirit?

How do all these things line up to David's prophecy in Tanakh, Ketuvim, Book I, Miktam of David, Psalms 16:8-11?

Who is the right hand of God?

Who is the Holy One who will not suffer decay?

Did you understand Amy's interpretation of Tanakh, Nevi'im, Zechariah 12:10?

They'll look on Me, God, the one giving the prophecy to Zechariah. The one they've pierced, God telling us He'll be pierced which is crucified Yeshua, which is God incarnate. And they'll mourn for Him as one mourns for an only child, which is God's flesh of Himself called the Son of God, Jesus. And grieve bitterly for Him as one grieves for a firstborn son, is Yeshua, the son of the Virgin Mary, God's only Son.

Day 4

Finish reading the last chapters of The Library Room

Do you believe everyone has a purpose here on Training Camp Earth?

Do you feel evil people serve a purpose in teaching others around them how not to behave?

How often do you refer to commentary when reading the Tanakh or Holy Bible?

Have you ever used the Talmud notes or Mishnah (Gemara) or Midrashim?

Would you consider using the Midrashim in the future for research pertaining to the Tanakh/Old Testament?

Do you serve God to gain spiritual crowns of glory *or* do you serve without expecting rewards and let the favor of God be upon you?

How do you feel about celebrating Sukkot by building a Sukkah?

How is this similar to Thanksgiving being celebrated in America or other nations?

Drew shared the thirteen principals of faith written by Maimonides. What are your current principals of faith according to your religious beliefs? (Call your church and ask if you don't know.)

Did you know, or remember seeing the "Thirteen Principals of Faith" before this question was asked?

How are they different than the ones written by Maimonides?

Do Jewish people have to forfeit all they know as being Jewish to become Christian?

Do they have to change their Shabbat/Sabbath to Sundays instead of Saturdays?

Do they have to give up celebrating traditional Holy days?

Do you feel the Messianic church is a trend Christians are dabbling in to feel more like "Hebrews - God' chosen people?"

What about the former Judaic members; are they attending so they feel like they're still being Jewish?

Is it possible the Messianic church is full of Jewish people believing in Yeshua but not wanting to completely give up their cultural traditions?

Is it possible the Messianic church movement provides a bridge for the two faiths to meld together?

How hard would it be to convert your cultural traditions to the other faith at this point?

Are you aware of any Messianic churches in your area?

I've noticed in several cities many traditional Christian churches are now hosting Messianic services on Saturdays. Search your directories to find and write down a Messianic church nearest you.

Are Jews who believe in Yeshua as their Mashiach still Jewish? If yes, how?

Are Drew's fears of being shunned by the Jewish community at his future place of employment real?

Can you relate to Jessica's disappointments in life?

Write your own list of disappointments in life.

Have you ever been depressed to the point of contemplating suicide?

How did/do you work through your troubled mind?

Have you ever felt the devastation of losing a loved one to suicide?

How have you worked through the pain of that loss?

In light of recent events involving celebrities committing suicide, and bringing to light the chemical imbalances that may be causing their depression, I pray those in need seek help.

If you are aware of someone who suffers from this disease, write their name here (including your own if that is the case too.) Pray for them whenever you think about them. Pray God sends them peace and comfort as they struggle with their bouts.

I found this web site blog informative. It is from a man who not only suffers from depression but lost a daughter to it as well. Please keep Eric Meyer in your prayers as well as those who suffer from this lying disease.

http://meyerweb.com/eric/thoughts/2014/08/11/depression/

Here is the web site to the International Association for Suicide Prevention – Resource Crisis Centers

http://www.iasp.info/resources/Crisis_Centres/

I agree with Eric Meyer. This disease is a liar; lying to its victims telling them they are useless and hopeless. If you are a victim of depression, don't believe those lies! You are loved, you are worth it, and there is immediate help for you right this second.

Day 5

Write your own letter to God.

Like in the novel what were the results of the entire team regarding Yeshua being the Mashiach for both Jews and Gentiles? Yes Split No

How do you feel about sharing this interactive guide with your friends?

Thank you for taking the time to get to know the characters in The Library Room, as well as the people who committed themselves to working on this project with you. May God bless you and keep you in His loving arms. May He shine His light upon your hearts and empower the Holy Spirit to use you to minister to others the truth and good news. Amen.

New Testament, John 1:1$_{NIV}$ - In the beginning was the Word, and the Word was with God, and the Word was God.

About the Author

Kimberly Loving Ross is the Author of *The Library Room* published by Tate Publishing, released August 2014. Her attraction to studying God's words began in Junior High when her parents, at her request enrolled her into a small local Christian School.

She currently enjoys life coaching, participating in study groups, and entertaining at speaking engagements. She relaxes by driving to the mountains, eloquently wrapping gifts, and rough-housing with her three year old grandson.

Writing and biblical research had always been a hobby until she decided to pursue it as a career in 2011.

You may contact her through Facebook, Google+, Twitter, or through her web site: www.thelibraryroom.net

Feel free to ask her questions concerning the material covered in her novel and interactive guide, to arrange a speaking engagement, or attend her next book signing session.

How to receive

discounted pricing...

Churches, synagogues, schools, colleges, bookstores, and libraries, ordering 5 or more books of THE LIBRARY ROOM please contact Terry Cordingley at Tate Publishing.   For discounted pricing and drop ship arrangements. He can be reached via telephone 888-361-9473 or via email terry.cordingley@tatepublishing.net

If you contact me through my website after you've received your shipment, I'll send you the same number of interactive guides for the cost of shipping only.

Made in the USA
San Bernardino, CA
16 July 2016